Treasures

Sarah Klaiber
Illustrated by Jeffrey Scott Perdziak

Kevin W W Blackley Books, LLC
Copyrighted Material
Treasures

For information about this title or to order other books and/or electronic media, contact the publisher:
Kevin W W Blackley Books, LLC
Buffalo, NY 14215
www.kevinblackley.com
books@kwwilson.com

Artwork by Jeffrey Scott Perdziak

Library of Congress Control Number:
2016957547

ISBN:
978-0-99608395-9 Hardcover

Printed in the United States of America

To Mackenzie and Cameron:
you are my treasures.
Therefore, I am the richest girl in the world.

Some treasures sparkle.
Some treasures glow.

Some treasures lived
on big ships long ago.

Some treasures are earned.
Some treasures are won.

9

Some treasures are scratched
and are loud when they run.

Some treasures are bought.
Some treasures are found.

Some treasures smell pretty
and grow in the ground.

Some treasures prance.
Some treasures pose.

17

Some treasures bark
and have a wet nose.

Some treasures are dressed
in ribbons and lace.

Some treasures you
could never replace.

Some treasures are given
as a token of love.

Some are a gift
from the Heavens above.

But not all treasures sparkle.
Not all treasures shine.

Some treasures are dirty
most of the time.

Not all treasures are gold.
Not all are brand new.

Some make mistakes
and cry when they're blue.

Some treasures are big.
Some are small as a bug.

Some treasures smile
and giggle and hug.

Some treasures are young.
Some treasures have grown.

Just look around
and find one of your own.

About the Author

Sarah Klaiber has been writing poetry and music since the age of five. She composed her first song at ten and worked her way up to being offered a record deal in the early '90s. Since then, her heart led her down the path of marriage and motherhood, yet the passion for writing always remained. This book represents the legacy she wishes to leave for her children, with hopes it will be a reminder to appreciate the small things.

About the Illustrator

Jeffrey Scott Perdziak's talents allow him to work on many different projects, including wildlife art, portraits, comic book art, murals, T-shirt designs, and illustrations for children's books. His biggest work to date is the West Shore Railroad mural in Clarence, New York. He is also working on his own comic, called *The Menagerie – Unexplained Legends*.

CPSIA information can be obtained
at www.ICGtesting.com
Printed in the USA
BVOW10*1320051216

468385BV00008B/3/P